# ANIMALS NEED SHELTER

Rourke
Educational Media

A Division of
Carson
Dellosa
Education

MARLA CONN

# Photo Glossary

 **barn**

 **bear**

 **bee**

 **bird**

 **cave**

 **fish**

 **hermit crab**

 **hive**

2

 nest

 pig

 plant

 shell

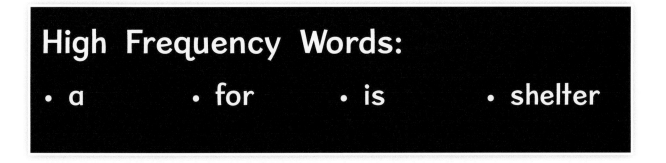

High Frequency Words:

- a
- for
- is
- shelter

3

A **nest** is shelter for a **bird**.

4

bird

nest

A **cave** is shelter for a **bear.**

cave

A **plant** is shelter for a **fish.**

plant

fish

A **shell** is shelter for a **hermit crab.**

shell

A **hive** is shelter for a **bee.**

hive

bee

A **barn** is shelter for a **pig.**

barn

14

pig

# Activity

1. Go back and read the story with a partner.

2. Discuss these questions:

   - Why do animals need shelter?
   - Where do animals live (habitats)?
   - How do animals survive in different habitats?

> ### *Teacher read-aloud:*
>
> *Animals need shelter to:*
> - *protect them from extreme weather.*
> - *hide them from predators.*
> - *help them find food.*

3. How do the following shelters help animals survive?

   **nest, cave, plant, shell, hive, barn**